Big Joy

Kay Gardiner and Ann Shayne

INTRODUCTION

THE FUNNY THING about giving is that it can warm the heart of both the recipient and the giver. That's what we're thinking about with this Field Guide.

The joy of giving.

More than 800 years ago, the Jewish philosopher Maimonides set out a way of thinking about charity that resonates today. His point: it's all good, and the less ego you have in it, the better.

Anonymous giving is big with Maimonides.

Knitting for others has a long, beautiful tradition in knitting, and everyone who has done it knows how it feeds the soul to make something for someone. It can be someone we love. Someone far away. Or someone we don't even know.

Give it away.

Give it to your sister, your friend at work, the guy without a hat you see on a corner on a cold day.

Tie a scarf to the back of a bench in the park with a tag saying "I'm not lost. If you're cold and need this piece of clothing to keep warm, please take it."

In this Field Guide, we welcome one of the biggest-hearted knitters we know, Jen Geigley.

Jen's specialty is quick knits that feel fresh and modern. We've got hats for every size head, one-size-fits-all cowls, a throw with afterthought bobbles, and a cozy cardigan. The yarn for all these projects? Rowan's Big Wool, a light and lofty yarn that comes in a great palette of colors.

This idea of giving is so contagious. We hope you'll join us as we make Jen Geigley's big knits and see how much joy we can launch into the universe.

Love,

Kay   Ann

BRAMBLEBERRY COWL

Design by

Jen Geigley

J EN KNOWS A THING OR TWO about cowls. Her Gaptastic Cowl is one of Ravelry's top ten most-knitted patterns. Ever. Like, almost 20,000 of them completed. It was the first pattern she ever posted on Ravelry or shared publicly anywhere, and in the decade since that fateful upload, Jen has continued to explore the cowl's potential virtually nonstop.

Her tried-and-true formula: choose a yarn and textured stitch pattern that drape well, make sure it is quick and fun to knit, and keep the look modern and versatile by sticking with solid colors and a long length that can be wrapped around the neck once or twice.

For the cushy cowl featured here, Jen chose the irresistibly squishy brambleberry stitch, which also goes by the names of bramble, cluster, blackberry, and raspberry.

KNITTED MEASUREMENTS

Circumference: 50" (127 cm)
Height: 13" (33 cm)

MATERIALS

— Big Wool by Rowan [100 g balls,
   each approx 87 yds (80 m), 100%
   wool]: 4 balls Golden Olive or Glum
— Size US 13 (9 mm) circular needle,
   32" (80 cm) long or longer, or size
   needed to achieve gauge
— Stitch marker

GAUGE

10½ sts and 14 rnds = 4" (10 cm) over
Brambleberry Stitch, after blocking
Note: For best results, wash the swatch,
pin it out when wet, then allow it to relax
for a day before measuring for gauge.

STITCH PATTERNS

1×1 Rib (even number of sts; 1-rnd repeat)
All Rnds: *K1, p1; repeat from * to end.

Brambleberry Stitch (multiple of 4 sts;
4-rnd repeat)
— *Rnd 1*: Purl.
— *Rnd 2*: *(P1, k1, p1) into next st;
   k3tog; rep from * to end.
— *Rnd 3*: Purl.
— *Rnd 4*: *K3tog, (p1, k1, p1) into next
   st; rep from * to end.
— Rep Rnds 1–4 for Brambleberry
   Stitch.

COWL

Using long-tail method, CO 132 sts. Join, being careful not to twist sts; pm for beg of rnd and work in the rnd as follows:

— Beg 1×1 Rib; work 4 rnds even.
— Change to Brambleberry Stitch; work Rnds 1–4 of pattern nine times.
— Purl 1 rnd.
— Change to 1×1 Rib; work 4 rnds even.
— BO all sts in pattern.

FINISHING

Weave in ends. Block as desired.

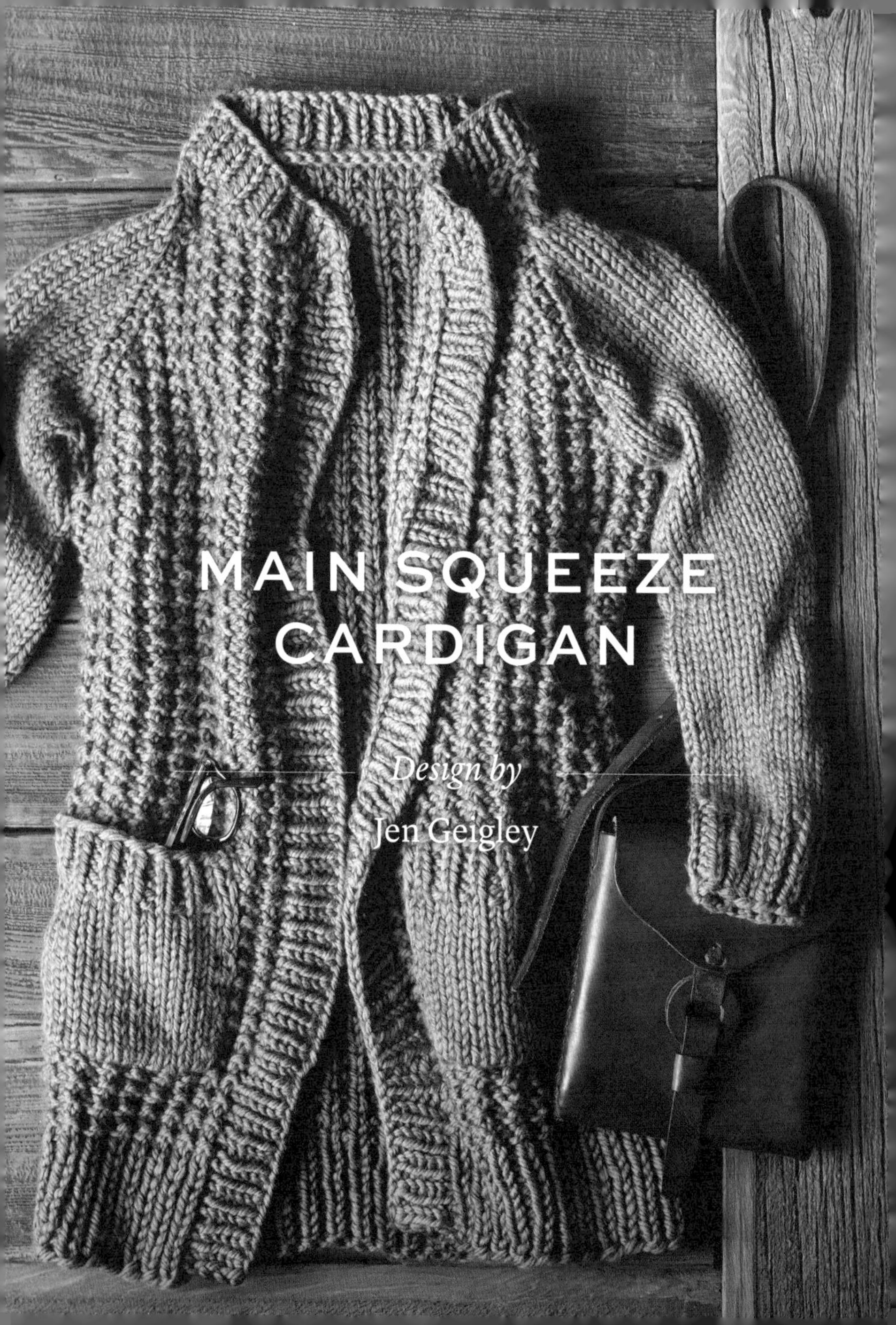

MAIN SQUEEZE CARDIGAN

Design by

Jen Geigley

T O JEN, WE SAID: please design a comfy cocoon of a cardigan that is a snap to knit and doesn't suffer from our pet peeve about big-stitch garments: I Feel Like I'm Wearing My Bathrobe Outdoors Syndrome.

Jen came through with her signature combination of elegance and playfulness. She matched a clean silhouette with a simultaneously cozy, chic, and fun-to-knit stitch pattern for the body, and then for the sleeves, she stuck with the closer fit of stockinette stitch. The front bands flow into an architectural collar, with no pesky fasteners.

When you think about it, at this gauge, your stitch count isn't that much higher than it would be for a traditional baby sweater, so go ahead and cast on for a garment that feels like a big, warm hug—a very special gift indeed.

KNITTED MEASUREMENTS

Bust: 39¼ (40¼, 43¼, 45) (46½, 48¼,
51¼) (53, 56¼, 57¾, 60¼)" [99.5 (102,
110, 114.5) (118, 122.5, 130) (134.5, 143,
146.5, 153) cm]
Length: 29½ (30½, 31¼, 31¼) (32¾,
32¾, 33¼) (34¾, 34¾, 34¾, 34¾)"
[75 (77.5, 79.5, 79.5) (83, 83, 84.5) (88.5,
88.5, 88.5, 88.5) cm]

SIZES

To fit bust sizes 37–39 (38–40, 41–43,
43–45) (45–47, 46–48, 49–51) (51–53,
54–56, 56–58, 58–60)" [94–99 (96.5–
101.5, 104–109, 109–114.5) (114.5–119.5,
117–122, 124.5–129.5) (129.5–134.5,
137–142, 142–147.5, 147.5–152.5) cm]

MATERIALS

— Big Wool by Rowan [100 g balls,
each approx 87 yds (80 m), 100%
wool]: 9 (10, 11, 11) (12, 12, 13) (14, 15,
15) balls Glum
— Size US 13 (9 mm) circular needle,
32" (80 cm) long or longer and
double-point needles (set of 4 or 5),
or size needed to achieve gauge
— Size US 11 (8 mm) circular needle 32"
(80 cm) long or longer, for picking up
sts for front bands and neckband
— Stitch markers

GAUGE

10 sts and 14 rows = 4" (10 cm) over stockinette stitch on US 13 (9 mm) needles
10 sts and 14 rows = 4" (10 cm) over Sand
stitch

STITCH PATTERNS

1×1 Rib (even number of sts)
— *All Rows/Rnds:* *K1, p1; rep from *
to end.

Sand Stitch (even number of sts)
— *Row 1 (RS):* *K1, p1; rep from * to
end.
— *Row 2:* Knit.
— Rep Rows 1 and 2 for Sand Stitch.

NOTES

The sleeves are worked in the round to
the underarms, then placed on hold while
the body is worked flat in one piece to the
underarms. The pieces are joined, and
the yoke is worked in one piece to the
end, with raglan shaping. Patch pockets
are knit and sewn on, and the front bands
and neckband are worked.

Underarm stitches are grafted together
using Kitchener stitch; if you prefer, you
may use 3-Needle BO.

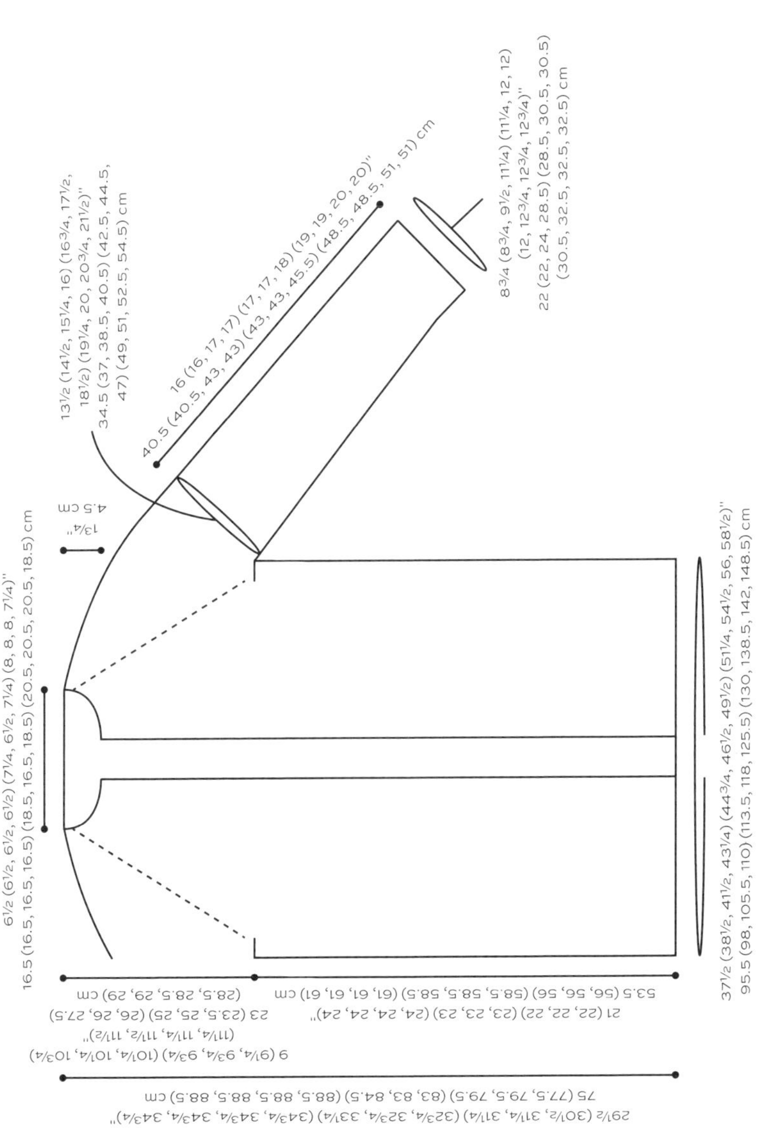
6½ (6½, 6½, 6½) (7¼, 6½, 7¼) (8, 8, 8, 7¼)"
16.5 (16.5, 16.5, 16.5) (18.5, 16.5, 18.5) (20.5, 20.5, 20.5, 18.5) cm
1¾"
4.5 cm
13½ (14½, 15¼, 16) (16¾, 17½, 18½) (19¼, 20, 20¾, 21½)"
34.5 (37, 38.5, 40.5) (42.5, 44.5, 47) (49, 51, 52.5, 54.5) cm
16 (16, 17, 17) (17, 17, 18) (19, 19, 20, 20)"
40.5 (40.5, 43, 43) (43, 43, 45.5) (48.5, 48.5, 51, 51) cm
8¾ (8¾, 9½, 11¼) (11¼, 12, 12) (12, 12¾, 12¾, 12¾)"
22 (22, 24, 28.5) (28.5, 30.5, 30.5) (30.5, 32.5, 32.5, 32.5) cm
37½ (38½, 41½, 43¼) (44¾, 46½, 49½) (51¼, 54½, 56, 58½)"
95.5 (98, 105.5, 110) (113.5, 118, 125.5) (130, 138.5, 142, 148.5) cm
9 (9¼, 9¾, 9¾) (10¼, 10¼, 10¾) (11¼, 11¼, 11½, 11½)"
23 (23.5, 25, 25) (26, 26, 27.5) (28.5, 28.5, 29, 29) cm
21 (22, 22, 22) (23, 23, 23) (24, 24, 24, 24)"
53.5 (56, 56, 56) (58.5, 58.5, 58.5) (61, 61, 61, 61) cm
29½ (30½, 31¼, 31¼) (32¾, 32¾, 33¼) (34¾, 34¾, 34¾, 34¾)"
75 (77.5, 79.5, 79.5) (83, 83, 84.5) (88.5, 88.5, 88.5, 88.5) cm

(handwritten:) Skein #1 — 4½"
#2 — 9"
#3 — 13½
#4 — 18"
#5 — 22"

SLEEVES *(handwritten: 1 skein each)*

Using larger dpns and long-tail method, CO 22 (22, 24, 28) (28, 30, 30) (30, 32, 32, 32) sts. Join, being careful not to twist sts; pm for beg of rnd and work in the rnd as follows:

— Beg 1×1 Rib; work 8 rnds even.
— Change to st st (knit every rnd); work 4 rnds.

SHAPE SLEEVE

— *Inc Rnd:* K1, M1L, knit to last st, M1R, k1—2 sts inc.
— Rep Inc Rnd every 7 (6, 6, 8) (6, 6, 6) (6, 6, 5, 5) rnds 3 (5, 1, 4) (1, 1, 5) (8, 8, 3, 9) time(s), then every 8 (7, 7, 9) (7, 7, 7) (0, 0, 6, 6) rnds 2 (1, 5, 1) (5, 5, 2) (0, 0, 6, 1) time(s)—34 (36, 38, 40) (42, 44, 46) (48, 50, 52, 54) sts.
— Work even until piece measures 16 (16, 17, 17) (17, 17, 18) (19, 19, 20, 20)" [40.5 (40.5, 43, 43) (43, 43, 45.5) (48.5, 48.5, 51, 51) cm], ending 2 (2, 2, 3) (3, 3, 3) (3, 4, 4, 5) sts before beg-of-rnd marker. Cut yarn and place next 4 (4, 4, 6) (6, 6, 6) (6, 8, 8, 10) sts on st holder or waste yarn (removing marker)—30 (32, 34, 34) (36, 38, 40) (42, 42, 44, 44) sts.

BODY

— Using larger circular needle and long-tail method, CO 94 (96, 104, 108) (112, 116, 124) (128, 136, 140, 146) sts.
— Beg 1×1 Rib; work 10 rows even.
— Change to Sand st; work even until piece measures 21 (22, 22, 22) (23, 23, 23) (24, 24, 24, 24)" [53.5 (56, 56, 56) (58.5, 58.5, 58.5) (61, 61, 61, 61) cm], ending with a RS row.

DIVIDE FOR FRONTS AND BACK

Division Row (WS): Work 21 (22, 24, 24) (24, 26, 28) (28, 30, 32, 34) sts for left front, work 4 (4, 4, 6) (6, 6, 6) (6, 8, 8, 10) sts and place on holder or waste yarn for underarm, work 44 (44, 48, 48) (52, 52, 56) (60, 60, 60, 58) sts for back, work 4 (4, 4, 6) (6, 6, 6) (8, 8, 8, 10) sts and place on holder or waste yarn for underarm, work to end for right front.

YOKE

— *Joining Row (RS):* Continuing to work in Sand st on back and fronts and st st on sleeves, work across right front sts, pm, knit across 30 (32, 34, 34) (36, 38, 40) (42, 42, 44, 44) sleeve sts from holder, pm, work across back sts, pm, knit across 30 (32, 34, 34) (36, 38, 40) (42, 42, 44, 44) sleeve sts from holder, pm, work across left front sts—146 (152, 164, 164) (172, 180, 192) (200, 204, 212, 214) sts.

— Work 1 WS row even.

SHAPE YOKE

— *Dec Row 1 (RS):* Continuing in established patterns, [work to 2 sts before marker, ssk, sm, k2tog] 4 times, work to end—8 sts dec.

— Rep Dec Row every RS row 10 (10, 11, 11) (12, 12, 13) (14, 14, 14, 14) more times—58 (64, 68, 68) (68, 76, 80) (80, 84, 92, 94) sts; 10 (11, 12, 12) (11, 13, 14) (13, 15, 17, 19) sts each front, 8 (10, 10, 10) (10, 12, 12) (12, 12, 14, 14) sts each sleeve, 22 (22, 24, 24) (26, 26, 28) (30, 30, 30, 28) sts for back.

SHAPE YOKE AND FRONT NECK

For Finished Bust Measurements 39¼ and 40¼" (99.5 and 102 cm):

— *Row 1 (RS):* BO 3 sts, [work to 2 sts before marker, ssk, sm, k2tog] 4 times, work to end.

— *Row 2:* BO 3 sts, work to end—44 (50, –, –) (–, –, –) (–, –, –, –) sts.

— *Row 3:* BO 2 (3, –, –) (–, –, –) (–, –, –, –)

sts, [work to 2 sts before marker, ssk, sm, k2tog] 4 times, work to end.

— *Row 4:* BO 2 (3, –, –) (–, –, –) (–, –, –, –) sts, work to end—32 (36, –, –) (–, –, –) (–, –, –, –) sts.

— *Row 5:* BO 2 sts, sm, [k2tog, work to 2 sts before marker, ssk, sm] 3 times, work to end.

— *Row 6:* BO 2 sts, work to end, removing markers—22 (26, –, –) (–, –, –) (–, –, –, –) sts; 1 st each front, 2 (4, –, –) (–, –, –) (–, –, –, –) sts each sleeve, 16 sts for back.

For Finished Bust Measurements 43¼, 45, and 46½" (110, 114.5, and 118 cm):

— *Row 1 (RS):* BO 3 sts, [work to 2 sts before marker, ssk, sm, k2tog] 4 times, work to end.

— *Row 2:* BO 3 sts, work to end—54 sts.

— *Row 3:* BO – (–, 3, 3) (2, –, –) (–, –, –, –) sts, [work to 2 sts before marker, ssk, sm, k2tog] 4 times, work to end.

— *Row 4:* BO – (–, 3, 3) (2, –, –) (–, –, –, –) sts, [work to 2 sts before marker, ssk, sm, k2tog] 4 times, work to end.

— *Row 5:* BO 2 sts, sm, [k2tog, work to 2 sts before marker, ssk, sm] 3 times, work to end.

— *Row 6:* BO 2 sts, work to end,

removing markers— – (–, 22, 22) (24, –, –) (–, –, –, –) sts; 1 st each front, 2 sts each sleeve, – (–, 16, 16) (18, –, –) (–, –, –, –) sts for back.

For Finished Bust Measurements 48¼, 51¼, 53, 56¼, 57¾, and 60¼" (122.5, 130, 134.5, 143, 146.5, and 153 cm):

— *Row 1 (RS):* BO – (–, –, –) (–, 3, 4) (3, 4, 5, 6) sts, [work to 2 sts before marker, ssk, sm, k2tog] 4 times, work to end.

— *Row 2:* BO – (–, –, –) (–, 3, 4) (3, 4, 5, 6) sts, [work to 2 sts before marker, ssk, sm, k2tog] 4 times work to end— – (–, –, –) (–, 54, 56) (58, 60, 66, 66) sts.

— *Row 3 (RS):* BO – (–, –, –) (–, 3, 3) (3, 4, 4, 5) sts, [work to 2 sts before marker, ssk, sm, k2tog] 4 times, work to end.

— *Row 4:* BO – (–, –, –) (–, 3, 3) (3, 4, 4, 5) sts, [work to 2 sts before marker, ssk, sm, k2tog] 4 times work to end— – (–, –, –) (–, 32, 34) (36, 36, 42, 40) sts.

— *Row 5:* BO – (–, –, –) (–, 2, 2) (2, 2, 3, 3) sts, sm, [k2tog, work to 2 sts before marker, ssk, sm] 3 times, work to end.

— *Row 6:* BO – (–, –, –) (–, 2, 2) (2, 2, 3, 3) sts, work to end, removing markers— – (–, –, –) (–, 22, 24) (26, 26, 30, 28) sts; 1 st each front, – (–, –, –) (–, 2, 2) (2, 2, 4, 4) sts each sleeve, – (–, –, –) (–, 16, 18) (20, 20, 20, 18) sts for back.

For All Sizes:
BO all sts.

POCKETS
(make 2)

— Using larger needle and long-tail method, CO 16 sts.

— Beg st st; work even until piece measures 6" (15 cm), ending with a WS row.

— Change to 1×1 Rib; work 6 rows even.

— BO all sts in pattern.

— Pin pockets to left front and right front so bottom of pocket sits approximately 8" above bottom edge. Sew pockets in place.

FINISHING
Block as desired.

Right Front Band

— With RS facing, using smaller circular needle and beg at lower right front edge, pick up and knit 66 (68, 72, 74) (76, 78, 86) (88, 88, 92, 92) sts along right front edge, or approx 2 sts in every 3 rows, ending with an even number of sts.

— Change to larger circular needle.

— Beg 1×1 Rib; work 1 row even.

- *Inc Row (RS):* Work to last st, M1L, k1—1 st inc.
- Rep last 2 rows twice more, working new sts into pattern—72 (74, 78, 80) (82, 84, 92) (94, 94, 98, 98) sts.
- BO all sts in pattern.

Left Front Band

- With RS facing, using smaller circular needle and beg at left front neck edge, pick up and knit 66 (68, 72, 74) (76, 78, 86) (88, 88, 92, 92) sts along left front edge, or approx 2 sts in every 3 rows, ending with an even number of sts.
- Change to larger circular needle.

- Beg 1×1 Rib; work 1 row even.
- *Inc Row (RS):* K1, M1R, work to end—1 st inc.
- Rep last 2 rows twice more, working new sts into pattern—72 (74, 78, 80) (82, 84, 92) (94, 94, 98, 98) sts.
- BO all sts in pattern.

Neckband

- With RS facing, using smaller circular needle and beg at right front neck edge (do not pick up in front bands), pick up and knit approx 34 (40, 36, 36) (36, 36, 40) (40, 44, 44, 44) sts along neck edge. *Note:* Exact st count is not essential; just be sure to end with an even number of sts.

— Change to larger circular needle.
— Beg 1×1 Rib; work 1 row even.
— *Inc Row (RS):* K1, M1R, work to last st, M1L, k1—2 sts inc.
— Rep last 2 rows twice more, working new sts into pattern—40 (46, 42, 42) (42, 42, 46) (46, 50, 50, 50) sts.
— BO all sts in pattern.
— Sew shaped edges of front bands to shaped edges of collar.
— With RS facing, join underarm sts using Kitchener st. If you prefer, you may join them using 3-Needle BO, as follows: Place underarm sts on 2 spare needles. Hold the sides with the RSs facing each other and the needles parallel. Using third needle and always working first st on front needle tog with first st on back needle, k2tog, *k2tog, pass first st over second st to BO 1 st; rep from * until all underarm sts are BO.
— Weave in ends.

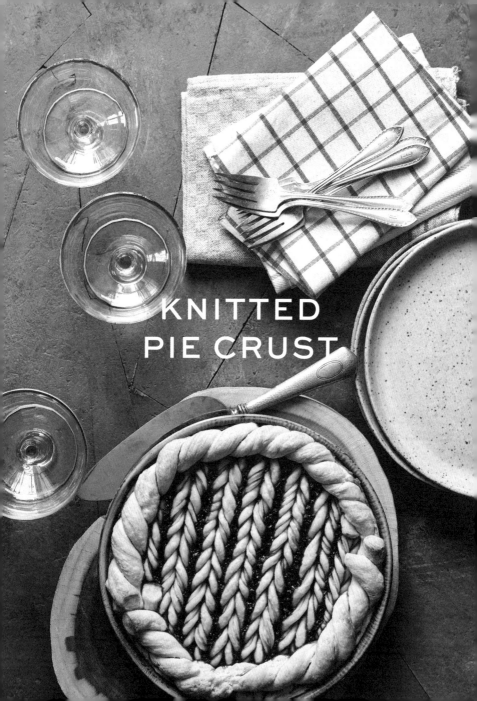

KNITTED
PIE CRUST

A KNITTED PIE CRUST? you ask. Yup. That's what we've got. Sort of. While we've heard of bakers literally knitting strands of dough, we like Jen's no-fuss adaptation that mimics the look of our favorite knit-a-row, purl-a-row stitch pattern. Here's the concept, which Jen came up with after spotting a similar version on craftberrybush.com.

Prepare your favorite fruit pie up to the point of making the top crust, then:

Roll out the crust dough (we use Trader Joe's, but homemade pie crust works great, too) and cut it into strips (using a pizza cutter if you have one). Roll each strip into a long snake, twist two snakes together (right over left), then place two pairs together across diameter of the filled pie. Repeat until the top is covered with faux stockinette stitch to your liking. If desired, twist together another two strands of dough, run around the edge of the pie, and smush together where they meet. (You're "knitting" in the round!)

Bake pie as called for in your recipe, keeping a close eye on the crust so that it doesn't brown too much.

STRIPEY
SCRAPPY
HATS

———— *Design by* ————

Jen Geigley

THERE ARE TIMES when we want to let loose and knit all the colors. Jen's Stripey Scrappy Hats, sized from baby to adult, scratch that itch with a design that invites easy experimentation. Knit with as many colors as you like. Work in neat stripes, or make it scrappy by changing colors mid-round, leaving the ends on the outside, like fringe. It's hard to go wrong when you're knitting at such a big scale. If a color suddenly looks out of place, you'll have only a few stitches to undo. Such a fine use for leftovers, this design. Even a small remnant can be part of the mix.

KNITTED MEASUREMENTS
Circumference: 14½ (16, 17½, 19¼, 22½, 24)" [37 (40.5, 44.5, 49, 57, 61) cm]

SIZES
Baby (toddler, preschool, child, adult S/M, adult L)

MATERIALS
— Big Wool by Rowan [100 g balls, each approx 87 yds (80 m), 100% wool]: 1 ball each

Striped Hat #1: two-color (page 32)
A: Smoky
B: Normandy

Striped Hat #2: multicolor (page 32)
A: Biscotti
B: Concrete
C: Pantomime
D: Prize
E: Smoky
F: Ice Blue
G: Mallard
H: Golden Olive

Scrappy Hat: multicolor (page 22)
A: Smoky
B: Golden Olive
C: Prize
D: Concrete

E: Vert
F: Glum
G: Pantomime
— Size US 13 (9 mm) circular needle, 16" (40.5 cm) long and double-point needles (set of 4 or 5), or size needed to achieve gauge
— Stitch markers

GAUGE
10 sts and 14 rnds = 4" (10 cm) over stockinette stitch

NOTES
This pattern may be worked in two-color stripes, multicolor stripes, or scrappy stripes where you change colors at random. Following the pattern is information on the stripe sequences used in the samples; work them as given here or create your own.

HAT

Using color of your choice and long-tail method, CO 36 (40, 44, 48, 56, 60) sts. Join, being careful not to twist sts; pm for beg of rnd and work in the rnd as follows:
— *Rnd 1:* *K1, p1; rep from * to end.
— Rep Rnd 1 four (4, 5, 5, 6, 6) more times.
— Change to st st (knit every rnd); work even until piece measures 4 (4½, 5, 5½, 6, 7)" [10 (11.5, 12.5, 14, 15, 18) cm].

SHAPE CROWN

Note: Change to dpns when necessary for number of sts on needle.
— *Dec Rnd 1:* *K7 (8, 9, 10, 12, 13) sts, k2tog, pm; rep from * to end, omitting final pm—32 (36, 40, 44, 52, 56) sts.
— Knit 1 rnd.
— *Dec Rnd 2:* *Knit to 2 sts before marker, k2tog; rep from * to end— 4 sts dec.
— Rep last 2 rnds 4 more times—12 (16, 20, 24, 32, 36) sts.
— Knit 1 rnd.
— *Dec Rnd 3:* *K2tog; rep from * to end—6 (8, 10, 12, 16, 18) sts. Cut yarn, leaving a long tail. Thread tail through rem sts, pull tight and fasten off.

FINISHING

Weave in ends. Block as desired.

TWO-COLOR STRIPE SEQUENCE

— CO and work ribbing in A.
— Work 5 (6, 7, 7, 8, 9) rnds in B.
— Work 1 (1, 1, 2, 2, 2) rnd(s) in A.
— Work 5 (6, 7, 7, 8, 9) rnds in B.
— Work 1 (1, 1, 2, 2, 2) rnd(s) in A.
— Work remainder of hat in B.

MULTICOLOR STRIPE SEQUENCE

— CO and work ribbing in A.
— Work 1 (2, 2, 3, 3, 4) rnd(s) in B.
— Work 1 rnd in C.
— Work 1 (2, 3, 2, 3, 4) rnd(s) in D.
— Work 1 (1, 1, 1, 1, 2) rnd(s) in E.
— Work 1 (2, 2, 2, 3, 3) rnd(s) in F.
— Work 1 rnd in G.
— Work 1 (2, 3, 5, 5, 6) rnd(s) in H.
— Work remainder of hat in E.

MULTICOLOR SCRAPPY SEQUENCE

CO and work ribbing in A. Change colors (A-J) at random (such as every few stitches, half rnd, 1½ rnds, and/or 2½ rnds, etc.) through remainder of hat.

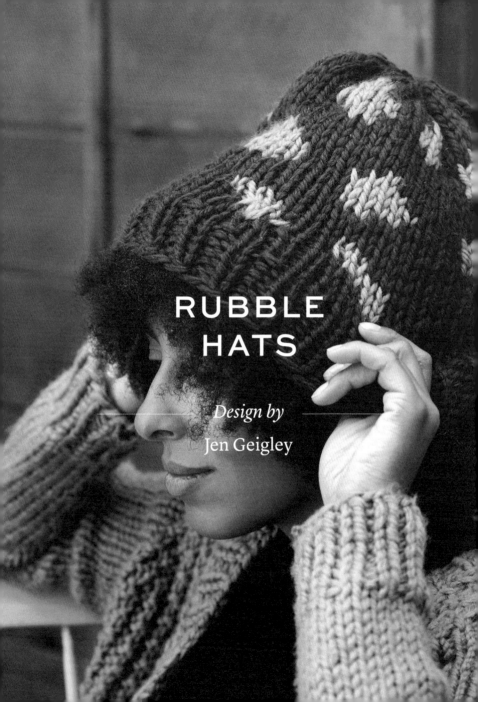

RUBBLE HATS

Design by

Jen Geigley

27

J EN IS A MASTER at mixing austere modernism and anime whimsy. When she showed us this design, with its stone-shaped dots, we laughed and immediately dubbed it the Flintstones Hat. Later, sample knitter Nell Ziroli started referring to it as the Rubble Hat, and Nell's name stuck.

Stranded colorwork at three stitches to the inch is not only fun—and fast—to knit, it creates a double thickness that reinforces the shape of the hat and gives it a millinery heft. In the right palette, it will fit right in with a sophisticated, citified wardrobe. And with giving in mind, it is sized for the modern stone-age family, including even Pebbles and Bamm-Bamm.

KNITTED MEASUREMENTS

Circumference: 14½ (16, 17½, 19¼, 22½, 24)" [37 (40.5, 44.5, 49, 57, 61) cm]

SIZES

Baby (toddler, preschool, child, adult S/M, adult L)

MATERIALS

— Big Wool by Rowan [100 g balls, each approx 87 yds (80 m), 100% wool]: 1 ball each

Colorway #1 (page 26)

A: Blue Velvet

B: Normandy

Colorway #2 (pages 30–31)

A: Cactus

B: Golden Olive

— Size US 13 (9 mm) circular needle, 16" (40.5 cm) long and double-point needles (set of 4 or 5), or size needed to achieve gauge

— Stitch markers

GAUGE

10 sts and 14 rnds = 4" (10 cm) over stockinette stitch

HAT

Using A and long-tail method, CO 36 (40, 44, 48, 56, 60) sts. Join, being careful not to twist sts; pm for beg of rnd and work in the rnd as follows:

— *Rnd 1:* *K1, p1; rep from * to end.

— Rep Rnd 1 four (4, 5, 5, 6, 6) more times.

— Change to St st (knit every rnd); knit 1 rnd.

— Work Rnds 1-16 (20, 21, 27, 28, 30) of Hat Chart, working outlined rep as indicated for your size.

— Knit 1 (1, 0, 1, 0, 1) rnd(s); piece should measure approx 6½ (7¼, 7½, 9½, 9¾, 10½)" [16.5 (18.5, 19, 24, 25, 26.5) cm].

SHAPE CROWN

Note: Change to dpns when necessary for number of sts on needle.

— *Dec Rnd:* *K2tog; rep from * to end—18 (20, 22, 24, 28, 30) sts.

— Knit 1 rnd.

— Rep Dec Rnd once more—9 (10, 11, 12, 14, 15) sts.

— Cut yarn, leaving long tail. Thread through rem sts, pull tight; fasten off.

FINISHING

Weave in ends; block as desired.

Hat Chart

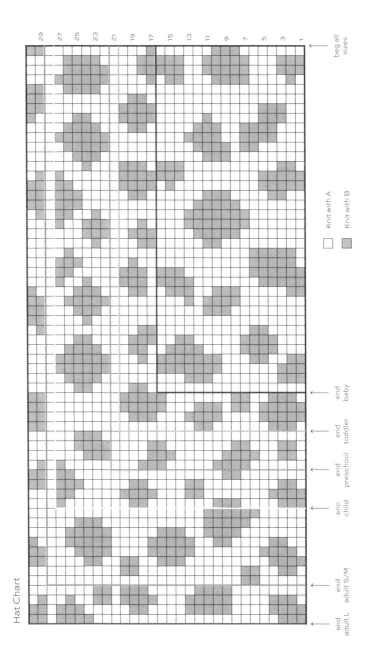

	Knit with A
	Knit with B

beg all sizes

end baby

end toddler

end preschool

enc child

end adult S/M

end adult L

29 27 25 23 21 19 17 15 13 11 9 7 5 3 1

O N SUMMER TUESDAYS, when I can, I head to New York's Bryant Park, where my local yarn shop, Knitty City, hosts a weekly outdoor knit-in. They provide lessons, needles, and yarn to all who want to learn. It's a jolly lunch-hour mix of beginners and experienced knitters, friends and strangers. What do we make? Scarves. Plain and fancy, knit and crochet, wool, cotton, and acrylic. Just: scarves.

This gathering of kindly urbanites would be enough in itself, but then, many weeks later, something happens to the scarves. Volunteers tag them: "Found but not lost—please take me if you are cold or give me to a person in need." And on a chilly winter day, dozens of folding chairs in Bryant Park are draped with these scarves. It's a beautiful sight, bright pops of color against green paint. It's like yarn bombing, but its purpose is to warm people.

Halfway across the country in Iowa, Jen Geigley is doing something similar. When winters are extra cold, she has been known to leave warm knitted accessories on benches near the library downtown, each one tagged with her I'm Not Lost tags, as shown here. Somewhere in Maimonides's hierarchy of giving—very high up—is charity that does not embarrass the recipient. When something is freely offered to all, there is only joy in receiving it, no questions asked. To download a full set of Jen's tags, go to tinyurl.com/ImNotLostTags.

—Kay

BOBBLE THROW

Design by

Jen Geigley

W E LOVE A BLANKET. While we've often said a handknit blanket is a form of immortality, it's also true that knitting one can seem to take an eternity.

What if the stitches were REAL BIG? Then we could knit blankets whenever we needed a superspecial baby or wedding gift or something to give to the blanket drive at our school or gym.

The simplicity of this stockinette blanket is deceptive. The opportunities for inventiveness are many. Jen's witty bobbles, which are added after the blanket has been knitted, are just a start. We're dreaming of versions that are colorblocked, striped, and scraptastic. And don't get us going on intarsia; this blanket is the perfect canvas for a big ol' smiley face or heart.

40" wide x 50" long (101.5 cm x 127 cm)

— Big Wool by Rowan [100 g balls, each approx 87 yds (80 m), 100% wool]: 20 balls Concrete (A); 4 balls Smoky (B); 1 ball each Golden Olive (C), Mallard (D), Pantomime (E), and Surf (F)
— Size US 13 (9 mm) circular needle, 32" (80 cm) long or longer, or size needed to achieve gauge
— Removable stitch markers or waste yarn

10 sts and 14 rows = 4" (10 cm) over stockinette stitch

Blanket body is worked in stockinette stitch, then mitered borders are picked up and worked in garter stitch, and the edges are sewn together. The after-thought bobbles are added after the blanket has been blocked.

— Using A and long-tail method, CO 90 sts.
— Beg st st (knit 1 row, purl 1 row); work even until piece measures 46" (117 cm), ending with a WS row.
— BO all sts.

Mitered Border
— With RS facing, using B, pick up and knit 1 st for every st along the CO edge.
— *Row 1 (WS):* Knit.
— *Row 2:* K1, M1R, knit to last st, M1L, k1—2 sts inc.
— Rep Rows 1 and 2 three more times, then rep Row 1 once more.
— BO all sts knitwise.
— Rep for BO edge, then rep for side edges, picking up and knitting approx 2 sts in every 3 rows.
— Sew shaped edges of borders together.
— Weave in ends; block as desired.

Afterthought Bobbles
— Using diagram as a guide, mark locations of bobbles on body of blanket with removable st markers or waste yarn, as follows: Place

| 37

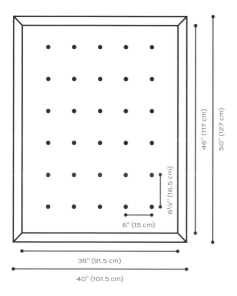

6 rows of 5 markers each; space markers every 6½" (16.5 cm) across the width of the body and every 5¾" (14.5 cm) down the length. If the body of your blanket is not the same width and/or length as given here, divide the body width by 6 and the body length by 7, and place markers accordingly. Take care to align markers along the same knitted row horizontally and the same knitted column vertically.

— With RS facing, using B, pick up and knit 1 st at first marker.

— *Row 1 (RS):* Knit into front, back, front, back, then front of st—6 sts.

— *Row 2:* Purl.

— *Row 3:* Knit.

— *Rows 4 and 5:* Rep Rows 2 and 3.

— *Row 6:* *Slip second st on right needle over first; rep from * until 1 st rem.

— Fasten off last st. Thread tail back down through bobble, then to WS of blanket; tie tails together to secure, and weave in ends.

— Rep for remaining bobbles in Colors C-F.

ABBREVIATIONS

Approx: Approximately
Beg: Begin(ning)(s)
BO: Bind off
CO: Cast on
Dec: Decreas(ed)(es)(ing)
Dpn: Double-pointed needle(s)
Inc: Increas(ed)(es)(ing)
K: Knit
K2tog: Knit 2 stitches together. One stitch has been decreased.
M1L: (make 1 left) Insert left needle from front to back under horizontal strand between stitch just worked and next stitch on left needle. Knit this strand through back loop. One stitch has been increased.
M1R: (make 1 right) Insert left needle from back to front under horizontal strand between stitch just worked and next stitch on left needle. Knit this strand through front loop. One stitch has been increased.

P: Purl
P2tog: Purl 2 stitches together. One stitch has been decreased.
Pm: Place marker
Rep: Repeat(ed)(ing)(s)
Rnd(s): Round(s)
RS: Right side
Sm: Slip marker
Ssk: Slip 1 stitch knitwise, slip 1 stitch purlwise, insert left needle into the front of these 2 stitches and knit them together from this position. One stitch has been decreased.
Ssp: Slip 2 stitches 1 at a time knitwise, slip them back to the left needle in their new orientation, purl them together through the back loops. One stitch has been decreased.
St st: stockinette stitch
St(s): Stitch(es)
Tog: Together
WS: Wrong side
Wyib: With yarn in back
Wyif: With yarn in front

MEET JEN GEIGLEY

Jen was launched into the knitting strato-sphere in 2010, when she quietly posted her first pattern on Ravelry, and quickly it became one of the most knitted projects on the site. Since then she has contrib-uted sweater and accessory designs to magazines, including *Knit Simple*, *Noro*, and *Knitsy*, and self-published six pattern collections—and counting. She became a Rowan ambassador in 2013 and in 2019, her book *Rowan Modern Family Knits* was published by Quail Studio. She's also a mom, a graphic designer, and popular knitting teacher in elementary and high schools in Des Moines, Iowa.

How did you come to knitting?
Art and design have been a huge part of my daily life since I was a child, and most everything I do stems from a love for art. I have a bachelor's degree in fine arts and graphic design. I learned to knit in 2008 and quickly became interested in learn-ing everything I could about knitwear, patterns, and construction. When I put my love for graphic design and knitting together, the stars aligned.

How does being a graphic designer inform your knitwear design?
My graphic design education/training taught me to start with a concept and to embrace process. I am able to do hands-on creative work with my knitted samples, art direct photo shoots, then design my books, and send the computer files to the printer. Very DIY, and maybe even a tiny bit punk rock.

What inspires your style?
I like going to art museums and concerts and also observing people on the street. I listen to a variety of music, especially when I'm working, everything from metal to punk to alternative. It's cold where I live so I design a lot of warm, cozy clothing I want to wear.